Designed For Success

Racing Cars

Revised & Updated

Ian Graham

www.heinemann.co.uk/library
Visit our website to find out more information about **Heinemann Library** books.

To order:
☎ Phone 44 (0) 1865 888066
🖹 Send a fax to 44 (0) 1865 314091
💻 Visit the Heinemann Bookshop at www.heinemann.co.uk/library to browse our catalogue and order online.

First published in Great Britain by Heinemann Library, Halley Court, Jordan Hill, Oxford, OX2 8EJ, part of Harcourt Education. Heinemann is a registered trademark of Harcourt Education Ltd.

© Harcourt Education Ltd 2008
The moral right of the proprietor has been asserted.

Editorial: Andrew Farrow and Dan Nunn
Design: Steven Mead and Geoff Ward
Illustrations: Geoff Ward
Picture Research: Melissa Allison
Production: Alison Parsons

Originated by Modern Age
Printed and bound in China by South China
    Printing Company

ISBN 978 0 431 16581 3 (hardback)
13 12 11 10 09 08
10 9 8 7 6 5 4 3 2 1

ISBN 978 0 431 16589 9 (paperback)
13 12 11 10 09 08
10 9 8 7 6 5 4 3 2 1

British Library Cataloguing-in-Publication Data
Graham, Ian, 1953 –
    Racing Cars. – (Designed for success) 2nd edition
    1. Automobiles, Racing – Juvenile literature
    I. Title
    629.2'28
A full catalogue record for this book is available from the British Library.

Acknowledgements
The publishers would like to thank the following for permission to reproduce photographs:
© Auto Cars p. **28**; © Jeff Burk p. **23** (bottom); © Corbis p. **25** (bottom); © Corbis/Ben Wood p. **19**; © Corbis/epa/Jaro Munoz p.**10** and title; © Corbis/epa/Kerim Okten p. **16**; © Corbis/epa/Rafael Diaz p. **20**; © Corbis/HOCH ZWEI / Michael Kunkel/New Sport p. **14**; © Corbis/Juergen Tap/Hoch Zwei/NewSport p. **12**; © Corbis/Pierre Minier - Ouest Medias/epa pp. **5** (top), **19**; © Corbis/REUTERS/ Christinne Muschi p. **24**; © Crash Media Group/Peter J Fox p. **15**; © Eye Ubiquitous/Darren Maybury p. **18**; © Getty Images p. **21** top; © Getty Images/Gavin Lawrence pp. **6, 7**; © Getty Images/Mark Thompson p. **13**; © LAT p. **13** top; © LAT/Lorenzo Bellanca p. **4**; © LAT/Charles Coates pp. **8, 25a**; © LAT/Charles Rose p. **9** (top); © National Hotrod Association pp. **22, 23** (top); © National Motor Museum pp. **26, 27** (top), **29**; © PA Photos/Manu Fernandez p. **11**; © Popperfoto p. **21** (bottom); © PowerStock p. **5** (bottom); © Sutton Images pp. **9** (bottom), **27** (bottom).

Cover photograph of the Formula 1 Grand Prix of Brazil reproduced with permission of © Getty Images/Paul Gilham.

Background images reproduced with permission of © istockphoto.com and © Corbis.

Every effort has been made to contact copyright holders of any material reproduced in this book. Any omissions will be rectified in subsequent printings if notice is given to the publishers.

Disclaimer
All the Internet addresses (URLs) given in this book were valid at the time of going to press. However, due to the dynamic nature of the Internet, some addresses may have changed, or sites may have ceased to exist since publication. While the author and publishers regret any inconvenience this may cause readers, no responsibility for any such changes can be accepted by either the author or the publishers.

 Contents

Any words appearing in the text in bold, **like this**, are explained in the Glossary.

Racing cars

People have raced cars for more than 100 years. Since the very first race, designers and engineers have tried everything to make their cars go faster than all the others.

A racing car not only has to **accelerate** very quickly, it also has to remain **stable** at all speeds and corner fast without skidding or spinning. In search of faster acceleration and higher speeds, designers develop new engines, use new materials, and try different body shapes. Compared to a family car, a racing car usually has a more powerful engine, a lower, more lightweight body, a sleeker shape, and bigger rear tyres. It also **handles** better than a family car. Many of the best racing car design ideas, including improved engines, brakes, and tyres, are later built into ordinary family cars.

Single-seaters ▽

International single-seat racing is divided into different classes, or formulas. These include **Formula 1** (shown here), **GP2**, and **Formula 3**. The "formula" is a list of rules covering the car's size, weight, engine, and **fuel**. The formulas are intended to make sure that all the cars in a race are similar to each other and so the race will be exciting to watch.

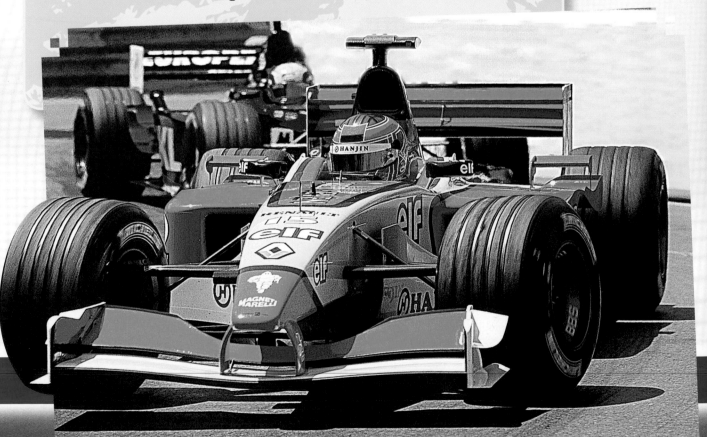

Sports cars △

The term "sports car" can be used to describe a range of cars. Some sports cars are passenger cars that are designed to be fun to drive on the open road. They have more power for their weight and better handling than the average passenger car. Other sports cars are used specially for racing. Some are almost identical to road-going models. Others are racing versions of road cars. They look like road cars, but have been completely rebuilt to be faster. There are also high-tech sports cars designed from scratch as ultra-fast racing cars.

Saloons and stocks ▷

Saloon cars are also known as "touring cars", "stock cars", or "sedans". There are races for saloon cars.

■ Some racing saloon cars are almost standard models. The only difference is that they carry some extra safety equipment.

■ Other racing saloon cars look like standard **production cars**, but underneath their familiar-looking body they are specially built racing machines.

Rule-makers

The rules and regulations for each type of motor racing are set by organizations or governing bodies. The Fédération Internationale de l'Automobile (FIA) regulates Formula 1 racing. The **National Association for Stock Car Auto Racing (NASCAR)** controls stock car racing in the USA. The **Indy Racing League** (IRL) is the organization behind IndyCar racing in the USA (see pages 6–7).

Indy cars

The IndyCar Series is the leading American single-seat, or open-wheel, motor racing sport.

An **Indy car**'s body is slung low between its wheels instead of sitting on top of them. The engine is placed in the middle of the car, behind the driver. The bigger rear wheels are driven by the engine, while the smaller front wheels steer the car. **Wings** at the front and back of the car create downforce, a force that presses the car against the ground and helps it to go round turns faster. To keep the car's body close to the ground, the driver sits low in the car in a seat that leans back in the **cockpit**. An Indy car weighs about half as much as a family car, but it has a far more powerful engine. This combination of its light weight, high **horsepower** engine, and **streamlined** shape enables an Indy car to **accelerate** from zero to 160 kph (100 mph) in less than three seconds. It can reach an amazing top speed of more than 355 kph (220 mph)!

Bank on it! ▽

Indy cars fight for position in a high-speed dash for victory. Many of the tracks they compete on in the USA are oval-shaped with banked corners. A banked corner rises up higher towards the outside of the corner. The banking enables the cars to corner much faster than they could on a flat track.

IndyCar races are fast and close-fought.

Fill her up! △

An Indy car takes on **fuel** through a hose that plugs into the car. A second hose at the top lets air and dangerous fumes out safely as fuel fills the tank. Indy cars do not burn ordinary petrol in their engines. Instead, they burn a type of alcohol called ethanol, which is made from plants. It is a more environmentally friendly fuel than petrol.

INDYCAR SERIES RACING CAR

Engine size: 3.5 litres

Engine type: V8

Engine power: 650 hp

Length: 3.0 metres

Weight: at least 694 kg (oval tracks)
at least 725 kg (road tracks)

Top speed: 355+ kph (220+ mph)

Sprouting wings ▷

Single-seat racing cars have wings at the front and back. The wings are shaped like an aeroplane's wing. When an aeroplane's wings cut through the air, they force air to travel further and faster over the curved top than the flatter underside. This lowers the **air pressure** above the wing. This difference in air pressure above and below the wing sucks the wing upwards.

Racing car designers turned this special wing shape, called an aerofoil, upside down so that it sucks the car downwards. This produces downforce, which gives the car more grip so it can corner faster without skidding.

downforce pushes the car downwards

wing

Racing saloons

Racing versions of family cars compete with each other on the racetrack. In Europe and Australia, they're called touring cars or saloons. In the USA, they're called stock cars or sedans.

Racing saloons look like standard **production cars**, but many of them are rebuilt especially for racing. Inside, these cars look completely different from a family car. Nothing is fitted to the car that is not needed for racing. All the soft padding that normally lines the roof and doors is stripped out. There is only one seat, for the driver. Like all racing car drivers, saloon drivers wear a fireproof suit, helmet, and full racing harness, and sit inside a strengthened **roll cage** for protection. Strict rules apply to the cars that are allowed to enter the various saloon car races. The rules cover the design of the cars and the engines they can use.

Australian supercars ▽

In Australia, touring cars are called **V8** Supercars. The races are held between modified Ford Falcons and Holden Commodores. These 5-**litre**, 600+ **horsepower** racers reach top speeds of about 300 kph (185 mph). One of the V8 Supercar races is the famous Bathurst 1000. At 1,000 km, this race is so long that two drivers take turns to drive each car.

A pair of Holden V8 Supercars race to the finish line at Melbourne in Australia.

◁ German touring racers

Many countries have their own touring car championships. Germany has the Deutsche Tourenwagen Masters, or DTM for short. The Mercedes-Benz C-Class is the most successful car in the championship.

US super stocks ▽

NASCAR stock cars are quite unlike any road car. Each one is hand-built to particular requirements. Under the bonnet, there is an enormous V8 5.8-litre engine. On the roof, there are flaps that stand up if the car goes into a high-speed spin. They are designed to spoil the car's **streamlined** shape so that there is no danger of it taking off like an aircraft! The driver's side window is covered by nylon netting to stop wreckage from flying inside during a crash. The netting also keeps the driver's arms safely inside the car.

NASCAR RACING CAR	
Engine size: 5.8 litres	
Engine type: V8	
Engine power: 770 hp	
Length: 2.8 metres	
Weight: 1,542 kg	
Top speed: 340 kph (210 mph)	

McLaren MP4-22

MCLAREN FLAIR

The McLaren **Formula 1** racing team was formed in 1963 by New Zealand racing driver Bruce McLaren. Its drivers have won the Formula 1 world championship 11 times. Two drivers, Ayrton Senna and Alain Prost, won three championships each in McLaren cars.

McLaren built a new model of car, the MP4-22, for the 2007 racing season. It is the most advanced car the team has ever produced. The shape of its parts and the materials they were made from were carefully chosen to make the car as light and as **streamlined** as possible. The engine was specially designed for the car. The first step in the design process was to develop the car's shape using a CAD (Computer Aided Design) system. Then models and full-size cars were built and tested in a wind tunnel. Next, prototype (test model) cars were built and tested with the new engine. Finally, the racing cars themselves were built.

The MP4-22 is the 71st car built by McLaren for Formula 1 racing.

air intake

engine

cockpit

rear wing

rear-view mirror

side pod

front wing

Aerodynamics

The shape and **aerodynamics** of the MP4-22 were refined during months of tests in a wind tunnel. An aircraft engine blows air through the tunnel to **simulate** the car travelling at different speeds. **Sensors** all over the car show the forces that act on different parts of it. The way air flowed around every part of the new McLaren car was studied. Designers wanted to see if it could be improved by changing the angle of one part or the size of another. Even the shape of the driver's helmet was designed according to tests in a wind tunnel.

A Formula 1 car model is tested in a wind tunnel. All Formula 1 manufacturers, including McLaren, use wind tunnels to test the aerodynamics of their cars.

Powerplant

The McLaren MP4-22 is powered by a Mercedes-Benz engine. It's a **V8**, which means that it has eight **cylinders**. A computer, called an "engine management system", controls the engine to make sure that it always works at its best. Engineers can change the way the system runs the engine to suit the conditions at different racetracks.

CLOSER LOOK

11

McLaren MP4-22
MADE BY HAND

To make their Formula 1 car, the McLaren racing team has to assemble about 11,000 parts and more than a kilometre of wire!

Most family cars are made from steel. Formula 1 cars are made from materials, such as aluminium, **carbon fibre**, and **titanium**, which are lighter and stronger than steel. The most important part of the car is the carbon fibre 'tub' that the driver sits in for protection. Carbon fibre is strong and can withstand very high temperatures. For this reason it is also used to make parts of the car's braking system, which can reach 1,300° Celsius during a race. When most cars are built, they stay the same from then on. Formula 1 cars are constantly being altered to suit the conditions at different racetracks. The engine settings, **suspension**, **gearbox**, and **wing** angles are all changed to make the car as fast as possible.

Making an F1 car

Thousands of family cars are built on **assembly lines**, where robots often do some of the work. McLaren MP4-22s were each built by hand by a team of engineers. They work in a room almost as clean as a hospital operating theatre! The cars are re-built for each race and undergo final preparation in a garage beside the track, like the one shown here at Sepang, Malaysia.

Carbon fibre

Carbon fibre starts as threads of rayon, a man-made fibre usually used to make clothes. The rayon is heated to 2,600° Celsius to change it into carbon. The carbon fibres are woven together to make something that looks like black cloth. To make a car part, the cloth is laid in a mould, soaked with a liquid called **resin**, and cooked to harden the resin. The result is a material that, weight-for-weight, is five times stronger than steel.

A driver tries out a newly-made carbon fibre body part at a Formula 1 factory.

Sitting pretty

A Formula 1 racing car corners so fast that the driver is pushed sideways with a force up to five times stronger than gravity. A close-fitting seat is very important, to hold the driver steady during a race. In fact, each seat is moulded to the exact shape of the driver's back to make sure that it's a perfect fit.

CLOSER LOOK

McLaren MP4-22
BLUE LIGHTNING

A Formula 1 racing team like McLaren spends hundreds of hours testing a new car to perfect its **performance**.

The MP4-22 was thoroughly tested in wind tunnels and on racetracks so its designers and engineers could fine-tune it to get the best possible performance. However, the real test comes when a car has to race against other racing-cars. Two MP4-22s raced for the first time at the Australian **Grand Prix** in March, 2007. They came second and third. They had their first win in only the second race of the season, the Malaysian Grand Prix, with Fernando Alonso at the wheel. Alonso, world champion in 2005 and 2006, won again in Monaco. The team's other driver, Lewis Hamilton, won the next two races in Canada and the USA in his first season in Formula 1.

Pit stops

Formula 1 racing cars are designed to have their wheels replaced and **fuel** tank refilled in a few seconds. A stop for this during a race is called a **pit stop**. A trained crew of twenty or so people can fit four new wheels and refill the fuel tank in less than eight seconds!

Hot rubber

A car's tyres grip the track better when they are hot because the rubber softens as it warms up. Just before a race starts, the tyres are wrapped in specially made electric blankets. These bring the tyres up to the right temperature, about 90° Celsius. As the cars drive around the track to the starting grid, they swerve from side to side to keep the tyres hot. Spare wheels that will be fitted to the car during a pit stop are also heated beforehand to give maximum grip.

The race for data

During a race, each car sends information to its team at the trackside by radio. More than 200 sensors all over the car measure everything from the temperatures of various parts to the tyre pressures and engine speed. The information appears on banks of computer screens. Each team takes up to 40 computers to the track. The numbers and graphs that appear on their screens show the team precisely how well a car is performing. If anything worries them, they can talk to the driver about it by radio.

MCLAREN MP4-22 FORMULA 1 CAR

Engine size: 2.4 litres

Engine type: V8

Engine power: 700 hp

Wheelbase: 3.0-3.3 m

Weight: at least 600 kg

Top speed: 360 kph (225 mph)

CLOSER LOOK

Engines

A racing car engine works in the same way as a typical family car's engine, but a racing engine is lighter and more powerful.

In theory, a racing car engine does a very simple job. It burns **fuel** to release the **chemical energy** stored inside it. It then uses this energy to drive the car's wheels. In practice, racing car engines are amazingly complicated. They can have up to twelve **cylinders**, compared to a small family car's four cylinders. Each cylinder needs its own supply of fuel and air, and an electrical supply to make the sparks that **ignite** the fuel. **Valves** have to open and close dozens of times a second to let air in and waste gas out at precisely the right moment. Oil moves through the engine to make sure that all the moving parts slide easily, and water cools the engine. The whole process is controlled by a computer.

Where is the engine? ▽

Racing cars often have their engine behind the driver. Placing the engine in this position lets the designer make the front of the car lower and narrower, so that it's **streamlined**. It also puts the weight of the engine closer to the middle of the car, which makes the car easier to **handle**.

engine position

Suck, squeeze, bang, blow ▽

A racing engine works in a series of four steps. They are often called suck, squeeze, bang, and blow. As each movement of the piston is called a "stroke", this is also called the four-stroke cycle.

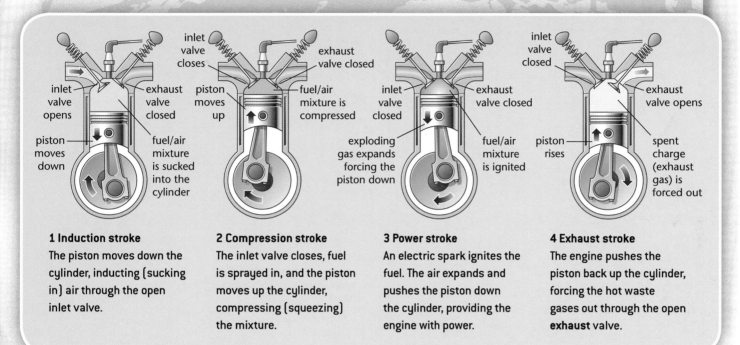

inlet valve closes

exhaust valve closed

inlet valve opens

inlet valve closed

inlet valve closed

inlet valve closed

exhaust valve closed

exhaust valve opens

piston moves down

exhaust valve closed

piston moves up

fuel/air mixture is compressed

inlet valve closed

exhaust valve closed

piston rises

fuel/air mixture is sucked into the cylinder

exploding gas expands forcing the piston down

fuel/air mixture is ignited

spent charge (exhaust gas) is forced out

1 Induction stroke
The piston moves down the cylinder, inducting (sucking in) air through the open inlet valve.

2 Compression stroke
The inlet valve closes, fuel is sprayed in, and the piston moves up the cylinder, compressing (squeezing) the mixture.

3 Power stroke
An electric spark ignites the fuel. The air expands and pushes the piston down the cylinder, providing the engine with power.

4 Exhaust stroke
The engine pushes the piston back up the cylinder, forcing the hot waste gases out through the open **exhaust** valve.

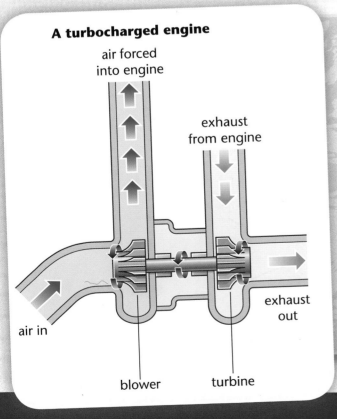

A turbocharged engine

air forced into engine

exhaust from engine

exhaust out

air in

blower

turbine

◁ Boosting power

Designers of racing engines try to squeeze as much power as possible out of their engines. Burning fuel faster produces more power, so racing engines are often designed to run faster than a normal car engine. When fuel burns, it combines with oxygen in the air. To burn more fuel, more oxygen may be needed. The most powerful engines force extra air inside them so that they can burn more fuel. These are supercharged or turbocharged engines. Engine designers have to stay within the rules of the sport. The rules may not allow power-boosted supercharged or turbocharged engines to be used.

Sports cars

Sports cars are small, low-slung cars built for speed and **manoeuvrability**. Some are designed to be driven on public roads. Others are specially designed for racing. They include some of the most beautiful racing cars that have ever been built.

The classic sports car for driving on public roads is a small, open-topped two-seater. Larger sports cars built for higher speeds, with an enclosed **cockpit**, are known as GT cars. GT stands for "*gran turismo*" or "grand touring". Sports and GT racing cars are two-seaters, although the passenger seat is not fitted. Classic sports cars have their engine fitted at the front, but most modern racing sports cars have their engine mounted in the middle of the car. Sports racing cars have become more and more sophisticated over the years. Changes in design have included lowering the front of the car, making the body more **streamlined**, adding a **wing** at the back, and replacing a lot of the metal parts with **carbon fibre**.

24 hours at the wheel ▽

The most famous sports car race is held every year near Le Mans in France. Most motor races are 2 or 3 hours long, but the Le Mans sports car race lasts for 24 hours. It's called an endurance race. A team of drivers take turns to drive each car. The leading cars can reach 320 kph (200 mph) on the circuit's long straights. Cars can average more than 200 kph (125 mph) over the whole 24 hours. In that time, the winning car can cover more than 5,000 kilometres. The cars have to be very reliable to run so fast for so long.

△ Le Mans American style

There is only one Le Mans 24-hour race, but Le Mans cars can now be seen in the USA and Canada in the American Le Mans Series (ALMS). The season begins with the 12-hour race at Sebring, Florida, but most of the races are 165 minutes long. The most successful ALMS cars are automatically invited to take part in the next Le Mans 24-hour race.

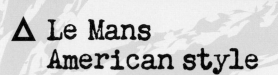

AUDI R10 LE MANS SPORTS CAR

Engine size: 5.5 litres

Engine type: V12 diesel

Engine power: 650 hp

Length: 2.98 metres

Weight: 925 kg

Top speed: about 350 kph (220 mph)

Classic ▷ racers

Old racing cars often find a new home in a museum when their racing days are over. Some of them carry on racing in events for classic cars. Graceful Jaguars from the 1950s and elegant Ferraris from the 1960s still take part in classic sports car races.

Rally cars

Rallying is one of the toughest tests of car and driver in motor sport. Rallies are held on closed roads and courses, called stages, set out in forests and parks.

A good rally car has to be an all-rounder — fast on the straights, quick and safe through the bends, and **stable** over the bumps. And it has to do all of this on all sorts of road surfaces. Rally cars race on **asphalt**, concrete, gravel, mud, and even snow and ice. The best rally drivers can reach an amazing 140 kph (85 mph) on a twisting, slippery, icy course. While the driver concentrates on driving the car, a navigator in the passenger seat follows a map of the course. He or she shouts instructions to the driver through an **intercom** system built into their helmets. The cars look like ordinary family cars, but they are actually hand-built from scratch and are far from ordinary.

Rock and roll ▽

Rally cars are probably more likely to end up upside-down than any other type of racing car. The driver and navigator sit inside a strong **roll cage**. This stops the roof from collapsing on them if the car rolls over. The cage is built from steel tubes welded together.

World Rally ▷ Championship

The cars that take part in the World Rally Championship are designed to be taken apart very quickly for repairs. Hitting a rock at high speed can shatter a wheel. However, the driver can fit a new wheel in less than five minutes. As soon as a car finishes a stage, a team of mechanics prepares it for the next stage. They can replace a part, even a major part such as a **gearbox**, within fifteen minutes.

FORD FOCUS WORLD RALLY CAR

Engine size: 2.0 litres

Engine type: 4-cylinder turbocharged

Engine power: 300 hp

Wheelbase: 2.64 metres

Weight: 1,230 kg

Top speed: 200 kph (125 mph)

◁ Tyre troubles

Rally teams choose from a variety of different types of tyres, depending on the weather and the ground conditions.

- On dry, hard surfaces teams choose tyres that are almost completely smooth — these allow the car to go faster.

- On loose surfaces, such as gravel, they choose tyres with a chunky, knobbly **tread** that gives more grip.

- For snow and ice, they fit tyres covered with steel studs or spikes, like the one on the left.

Drag racing

Drag racing is the fastest and most exciting motor sport on Earth. Racing a drag car, or dragster, is more like strapping yourself into a rocket than driving a car!

Dragsters are designed to cover a straight track, usually a quarter of a mile (402 metres) long, in the shortest possible time. They **accelerate** faster than any other racing car. There are more than a dozen different types, or classes, of dragsters. The fastest, called the Top **Fuel** cars, leave the start line faster than a jet fighter-plane! In less than one second, they are doing 160 kph (100 mph)! They have the most powerful engines in racing for punching their long thin bodies along the track. They measure their power in thousands of **horsepower**. The cars race two at a time against the clock. The noise, as they blast down the track, is deafening and the ground shakes. A whole race, from start to finish, lasts just a few seconds!

Fuel recipes ▽

Top Fuel dragster engines don't burn ordinary petrol. They burn a special fuel called nitromethane. Anyone working near a nitromethane car has to wear a gas mask because of the harmful fumes the engine produces. Apart from carbon monoxide, an invisible poisonous gas, it can also produce nitric acid – a strong acid that can even eat through metal.

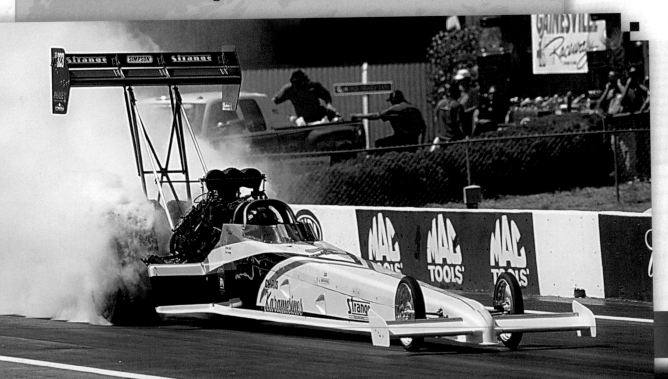

Keeping it ▷ straight

The design of a dragster makes it difficult to steer. When it roars away from the start line, the engine delivers so much power to the rear wheels that the front of the car tries to lift off the ground. Front wheels that are off the ground or that have very little grip cannot steer the car. If the nose begins to veer to one side, the force of the air suddenly hitting the side of the car can push it off-course in a moment.

Slowing down ▽

The fastest dragsters need more than brakes to stop them at the end of a race. As they cross the finish line, they release a parachute from the back of the car. The broad sheet of material catches the air, slowing the car down.

TOP FUEL DRAGSTER

Engine size: 8.2 litres

Engine type: V8 supercharged

Engine power: 7,000 hp

Wheelbase: 7.6 metres

Weight: 1,009 kg

Top speed: 525+ kph (325+ mph)

▷ Race safety

Safety is an important factor in the design of cars that race around a track at 350 kph (220 mph) or more. Every care needs to be taken to protect the drivers and the thousands of spectators who watch them.

Motor racing is a dangerous sport. If something goes wrong, it often happens in the blink of an eye and the result can be disastrous. Racing car designers have to follow specially developed rules. These try to make the cars as safe as possible. Modern racing cars protect their drivers better than ever. The driver sits inside a "survival cell". This is designed to withstand the enormous forces of a crash without collapsing or crushing the driver. The tracks are safer now, too. Many of them have wide "run-off" areas and soft barriers designed to catch cars that leave a track. Motor racing, though still dangerous, is probably safer now than it has ever been and it is just as exciting to watch.

The start of a race is particularly dangerous as the cars **accelerate** hard while very close together. Here, a car hits a wall at 290 kph (180 mph). The driver is so well protected that he suffers nothing worse than a sprained ankle.

Strapping in ▷

The driver is tightly strapped into his or her seat by a harness. If the car crashes, the harness ensures that the driver stays inside the car's survival cell and is not thrown out. The straps are held together by one fastener in the middle. This lets the driver release them all in a fraction of a second and escape if necessary.

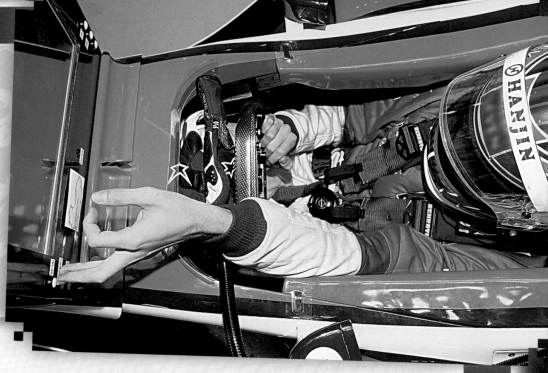

Safety standards

Thanks to modern safety standards, drivers can survive crashes that would have killed them just a few years ago. In the early days of motor racing, drivers sat in open **cockpits** without seatbelts. They wore cotton overalls that gave them no protection from the fires that often broke out after crashes. Many famous and successful drivers died on the track in those days. The **Formula 1** champion driver Jackie Stewart played an important part in making motor racing as safe as it is today.

Rubber tanks ▽

Racing cars are fitted with **fuel** tanks, called fuel cells, that look more like rubber bags. These strengthened bags are filled with plastic foam to stop the fuel from sloshing about or spraying out if the car crashes. **Valves** control the flow of fuel to the engine, and snap shut automatically to stop leaks. This greatly reduces the danger of fire.

During a **pit stop**, the fuel cells can be filled within 6.5 seconds.

Non-starters

All racing car designers are constantly looking for new ideas to give their team's cars the edge over all the others. Of course, some ideas are more successful than others!

Most new racing cars improve a little on other existing cars. However, from time to time, a designer tries something completely new to leap ahead of everyone else. Some new ideas, such as putting the engine behind the driver or using **wings**, work so well that other teams copy them. However, many other new ideas are quickly dropped or banned. Racing car designers, especially in **Formula 1**, play a cat and mouse game with the rule-makers. The designers constantly push technology to the limit to make their cars faster. Meanwhile, the rule-makers constantly update the rules. Their aim is to keep all the cars as safe as possible and make sure they all have roughly the same **performance**. Some new designs fail to catch on simply because they do not live up to the designer's hopes for them.

Jet-cars ▷

In the 1960s, several designers produced racing cars powered by **jet engines**. The first one nearly won the 1967 Indianapolis 500 race in the USA. The following year, the Lotus team raced four jet-cars in the USA. Two of them are pictured here. In 1971, Lotus also raced the only Formula 1 jet-car. The cars ran well at high speeds, but they could not **accelerate** as fast as other cars and the engines overheated when the cars slowed down.

◁ Six-wheelers

In 1976, the Tyrell Formula 1 team raced a car with six wheels. Two pairs of front wheels could be made smaller than one pair. Air flowed over the top of the small wheels more smoothly. However, both pairs of front wheels had to turn to steer the car. This made the front of the car very complicated and heavy. It failed to work as well as expected, and so the team went back to cars with four wheels the next year.

The fan car ▷

In 1978, the Brabham Formula 1 team built a car with a big fan at the back. The spinning fan sucked air from underneath the car to suck the whole car down closer to the track. However, cars were not allowed to have moving parts that changed the way air flowed around them. The fan seemed to break this rule. Drivers also complained that it sucked up dirt and blew it at following cars, so the fan car had to go!

Data files

Every racing car is designed with a particular type of driver or sport in mind. This table of information compares the basic specifications and **performance** of some of today's best-known racing cars.

Car	Engine	Power (horsepower)	Weight (kilograms)	Top speed (kph / mph)
Audi R10 Le Mans sports car	5.5-litre V12	650	925	350 / 220
McLaren MP4-22 F1 car	2.4-litre V8	700	600	360 / 225
IndyCar Series racing car	3.5-litre V8	650	694	355+ / 220+
NASCAR racing car	5.8-litre V8	770	1,542	340 / 210
Top Fuel dragster	8.2-litre V8	7,000	1,009	525+ / 325+
Ford Focus World Rally car	2.0-litre in-line 4	300	1,230	200 / 125

The first motor race

The first motor race was held in France in 1894. It wasn't supposed to be a race at all. It was called a trial. However, everyone wanted to know which car was the fastest. Count Jules de Dion's steam tractor won, but was disqualified. Next came Georges Lemaître in his Peugeot. The trial was so successful that a race was organized for the next year. Motor racing had begun.

This is a photograph of the Tour de France motor race in 1899.

Books

NASCAR, Rachel Eagen (Crabtree Publishing, 2006)
Racing Cars, Andrew Van de Burgt (J. H. Haynes, 2006)
Formula One, David Orme (Ransom Publishing, 2006)
Superfast Cars, Mark Dubowski (Bearport Publishing, 2005)
Indy Car Racing, Bruce Fish and Becky D. Fish (Chelsea House Publications, 2004)

Websites

http://news.bbc.co.uk/sport1/hi/motorsport/default.stm
BBC Sport's motorsport section, which includes news, facts, and features on motor racing and rallying.

http://www.nascar.com
The website of NASCAR, organizer of the US Winston Cup stock car championship.

http://www.indycar.com
The website of the IndyCar racing championship.

http://www.nhra.com
The website of the NHRA, organizer of US drag-racing championships.

http://auto.howstuffworks.com/nascar.htm
An explanation of how NASCAR racing cars work

http://www.themotorweb.com.au
A website full of useful information about all aspects of motor racing in Australia.

In 1959 the Cooper Climax was the first **Formula 1** car to have its engine behind the driver.

Glossary

accelerate go faster. To make a racing car go faster, the driver presses the accelerator pedal. This feeds more fuel into the engine, which speeds up.

aerodynamics the science of how objects move through air. It is used in motor racing to design a car shape that slices through air quickly.

air pressure the pressing force of the air around us. Racing car wings are designed to lower the air pressure below them and suck the car downwards.

asphalt a mixture of black, tarry bitumen and gravel, used to make roads

assembly line a line of machines where workers or robots put cars together

carbon fibre material made from strands of carbon embedded in hard plastic. It is a very strong and lightweight material that is used to make parts of some sports cars and racing cars instead of steel.

chemical energy the energy stored inside a chemical fuel such as petrol. The energy, released by burning the fuel, is used to make a car move.

cockpit the part of an aeroplane or car where the pilot or driver sits

cylinder tube-shaped part of a car engine where the fuel is burned

exhaust the waste gases produced when an engine burns fuel

Formula 1 (F1) the leading international single-seat racing championship

Formula 3 (F3) a class of single-seat motor-racing

fuel substance that is burned inside an engine to provide the energy that drives the car's wheels

gearbox part of a racing car that feeds the engine power to the wheels. The engine drives one shaft and the wheels are driven by another shaft. The two shafts are linked by a set of gear-wheels with teeth that lock together. When the driver changes gear, a different gear-wheel links the two shafts, enabling the engine to drive the wheels over a wide range of speeds.

GP2 international championship set up to give racing drivers experience in single-seaters before the best drivers move on to race in Formula 1

Grand Prix national race that counts towards an important championship such as the Formula 1 driver's championship

handling how a car responds and holds the road when it is being driven

horsepower unit of measurement of the power of an engine equal to the work done by one horse, or 746 watts of electrical power

ignite set on fire. The fuel inside an engine is set on fire by an electrical spark.

Indy car a single-seat racing car that takes part in IndyCar racing in the USA

Indy Racing League the organization that sets the rules and regulations for the IndyCar Series and Indy Pro racing in the USA

intercom a communication system that lets the driver and navigator hear each other over the noise of the engine

jet engines engines that work by burning fuel to create a high-speed stream, or jet, of gas, which makes a turbine spin. The turbine spins a fan that sucks air into the engine. Jet engines are also known as gas turbine engines.

litre measurement of capacity and a way of measuring the size of an engine. One litre is equivalent to 1,000 cc (cubic centimetres).

manoeuvrability the ability to be steered nimbly and sharply

NASCAR the National Association for Stock Car Auto Racing, which sets the rules for the Winston Cup stock car championship

performance the way a vehicle functions – its speed, acceleration, stability, etc.

pit stop a short visit to the pits, during a race. Cars may come into the pits during a race to have new wheels fitted, their fuel tanks refilled (if allowed), or damaged parts replaced.

production cars cars that are produced in large numbers for sale to the public

resin a liquid plastic used to make body parts of some racing cars. The plastic resin is poured into a mould. Mats of fibres made from glass or carbon are laid on top and soaked in the resin. When the resin sets, the result is a hard, smooth, and lightweight part.

roll cage a protective frame made from steel tubes welded together

sensor a device that detects and measures something

simulate to recreate the effect of something

stable steady. A stable car keeps steady at all speeds.

streamlined designed to move through air very easily

suspension the set of springs and other devices that connect a vehicle's frame to its axles. The suspension system lets the wheels follow bumps and hollows in the ground, while the rest of the vehicle moves along more smoothly.

titanium a strong, lightweight metal that does not rust

tread the outer part of a tyre that touches the road

valve part of a racing car that opens and closes to start, stop, and vary the flow of air, water, or fuel through the engine

V8 type of car engine. The number refers to the number of cylinders.

wheelbase the distance between a car's front and rear wheels

wings parts of a car shaped like upside down aircraft wings. As they cut through the air, they create a force that presses the car downwards.

Index

RACING CARS